In the Care of the Father

ॐ

Jan Pauley

In the Care of the Father
by Jan Pauley, Pensacola, FL 32533 (850) 937-9422

Printed in the United States of America

Library of Congress Control Number: 2002101011
ISBN 1-591600-12-X

Unless otherwise indicated, Bible quotations are taken from the New King James Version, copyright ©1982 by Broadman & Holman Publishers.

Xulon Press
11350 Random Hills Road
Suite 800
Fairfax, VA 22030
(703) 279-6511
XulonPress.com

Illustration by Carole Burke Garrison,
Pensacola, FL 32506 (850) 457-4144

Dedication

This book is written simply to stir the hearts of all that have accepted Jesus as their Savior and have allowed Him to be the Lord of their life. We each have a personal call on our lives to account for our relationship with God, our Heavenly Father, Jesus our Brother and Friend, and the Holy Spirit, our Comforter.

The only motive for sharing my thoughts is to encourage each believer to press on in his or her personal relationship with Jesus. I am not a theologian, but one who, from the very moment I accepted Jesus as my Savior, insisted I hear from Him in whatever circumstances arose in my life.

This book is dedicated to my husband, Nolan, who has certainly, "fought the good fight;" and our daughter Jo, a real comedian, who is sweet, tenderhearted and sensitive to the needs of others. Another who needs recognition for her encouragement is

Doris, a dear friend and balcony person who would always cheer us on no matter what. Evelyn, a dear friend, who always encouraged me to walk with Him. The three wise people, Brother John, Pastor Gary and Sister Mary. They were chosen to walk by my side. To the Brownsville Assembly of God congregation and Farmhill United Methodist Church for believing God's Word. And to the medical field at large – to those medical heroes who have truly dedicated their lives to help other people win the battle over death and defeat, I give thanks.

Foreword

༄

I John 5:7 –

> *For there are three that bare record in heaven, the Father, the Son and the Holy Spirit; and these three are one.*

Nolan and I are currently fulfilling a promise the Lord gave us eighteen years ago. Along with Nolan's work at Brownsville Assembly of God, on occasion we travel to other churches to help meet their audio needs. It is such a privilege to share what the Lord has given us with congregations all across the United States.

It has taken all these years for others to understand that Nolan's work with the audio is a ministry. He has always had this calling on his life and his talent came from none other that the Lord Himself. So then faith comes by hearing, and hearing by the Word of God – Romans 10:17. It only makes sense that God would fulfill His Word in every way.

Satan has fought hard over many years to deter us from our work for the Lord. But, greater is the Lord Jesus Christ who is in us than the devil who is in the world. With humble hearts we submit this book to your care. We pray the Lord's blessing upon you as you journey with us through these past years.

Romans: 15:13 - Now the God of hope fill you with all joy and peace in believing, that you may abound in hope, through the power of the Holy Ghost.

Because of Him,
Nolan, Jan and Jo Pauley

Contents

ॐ

Oh, For the Love
of Jesus

୬ଡ଼

It was a beautiful September day, September 11,
1977. The breeze was blowing the beautiful cumu-
lus clouds around the sky in Vinton, Iowa. It was
approximately 65 degrees. I was on my way to the
local Free Methodist Church where I had attended
regular services since moving to Vinton in July, for
an appointment with our young pastor, Pastor Bill.

While walking up to Pastor Bill's office, I remember wondering if this meeting would make a differ-
ence in my life. You see, I had been very despondent
for several weeks, even months. My move to Vinton
in July had once again taken me from family and
familiar surroundings. Looking back I can see God
was placing me where He could reach me. I was
twenty-six years old and I did not know Him. I made
every effort to quickly become familiar with my new

home and the people who were there. I had been attending this little church since July, participating in regular Wednesday and Sunday services as if I had always lived my life in church. I even shared an object lesson with Vacation Bible School children.

Pastor Bill was faithfully at his desk ready to assist one of his regular attendees. As I sat down, I began to share my feelings. Everything in my life was "OK", but I was experiencing a feeling of despondency – as if something was missing in my life.

Pastor Bill immediately began to ask, "Have you accepted Jesus as your Savior?"

My response was very sincere, "Of course I know Jesus. After all, I have attended church regularly on Christmas Eve and Easter."

Pastor Bill asked a second time, "Do you know Jesus as your Savior?"

Once again I responded cheerfully, "I know who Jesus is."

The third time Pastor Bill asked the same question, the Holy Spirit entered the room. His presence was undeniable. At that moment I was convicted. And in a moment of time what I had been searching for all of my life was revealed to me.

No longer in control, I began confessing my sins – naming them one by one – and recognizing my need to receive Jesus as my Savior. Tears of joy and relief fell from my eyes. Truly born again, I had come out of the darkness into the marvelous light and love of Jesus Christ!

It was like floating on air. My life-long search was over. I knew the void I tried so hard to fill was filled to overflowing with the Lord. If I had died that night I would have gone to Heaven to live with Jesus forever. Memories flooded my mind with the old gospel hymn we sang so often. Love lifted me, love lifted me, when nothing else could help, love lifted me. The angels rejoiced, but Satan was not happy.

Entering the
Throne Room of God

༄

Early in my walk with the Lord it was difficult to grasp the concept of God's love for me. I would often imagine Him in His throne room taking care of His business. While I, His daughter, waited with great expectation outside the throne room doors to be announced to Him, my mind could only imagine why He would entertain spending time with me. I knew I was His daughter, but He was God.

The foyer walls were draped with the most radiant purple and gold materials to be found. The doors that led into the throne room were magnificent beyond compare, laced with gold. The angels that stood on either side of the doors waited expectantly to open the doors and announce with trumpet my time to enter His presence. The moment was exhilarating, like nothing anyone could experience except with God.

My attire was Godly attire that would be expected of His daughter. The dress I wore was long and flowed elegantly to the floor. The train of the dress was made of a softer and sheerer material. It trailed gracefully behind me. My hair was soft and free flowing crowned with a ring of beautiful baby roses to complement the color of my cheeks.

The angels suddenly received their signal to sound the trumpets. The doors slowly, but surely opened as I dared take the first step to enter His presence. As I stepped, I stepped again with a quicker pace than the step before. Before I could think, I was gracefully running down the long walkway to His throne. I could see Him sitting there in all of His majesty. He was turned to the right side of His throne completing a conversation with one of His servants. As He sensed my presence He turned His head to gaze directly upon me. The sheer delight in His eyes at the sight of one of His children running to see Him brought the throne room attendants to their knees in awe of His brilliance.

I spoke, "Father!"

And He said, "Daughter, come quickly to my side."

I bowed in reverence to Him, and rose and sat at His side for a morning chat. We spoke briefly of the beautiful sunrise and how the dew sweetly kissed the flowers in the garden. He had plans for me today – special plans, just like each new day. Was I prepared to carry these special plans through? Only by His grace! He gently reminded me of His love for me and asked if there was anything He could do for me today.

I simply said, "Be with me, dear Father and guide me each step of the way!"

With a nod of His head, I stood and once again bowed in reverence to Him and left His presence.

Even the most difficult times, those times I felt most unworthy, I reminded myself that I was His daughter. How was I to dress? How was I to speak? What was my mission for the day? Always reminding myself of His presence and His peace.

The Goodness of God...

᨞

One month to the very day I accepted Jesus as my Savior and Lord, I was accidentally shot in my right leg. I was a teacher at the local junior high and had been home ill for two days. A friend was with me. He was experienced in handling guns so I thought nothing of him checking out his gun in my presence. I was in the living room half-sitting and half-lying down on my pull-out sofa. My friend's attention was on the gun he was examining. He looked down the barrel and pushed in and pulled out on what he thought was an empty clip.

At that instant, I heard a voice speak to me directly in a calm and reassuring manner. It was as if someone was standing behind me.

The voice echoed loudly and clearly, "Drop your legs." In slow motion, I managed to drop my left leg.

As the gunshot rang loud in my small apartment, my body, which was now parallel to the sofa bed, shot three feet into the air.

I landed safe on the sofa and simply stated, "You have shot me!"

There was a half-inch diameter of blood shooting from my inside right leg. I began to compress the area with my hands while encouraging and instructing my friend to get me a towel so I could make a tourniquet. Needless to say he was panicked. I wrapped my leg while he called 911. In a rather hysterical manner, he confessed to accidentally shooting me in the leg.

It seemed like an eternity passed by before the policeman arrived at my apartment door. As the policeman entered my apartment, I panicked. I reached out my hand and asked him to please help me. The ambulance arrived and as they put me on the stretcher, I asked for my Bible. During the ride in the ambulance, I clung very tightly to my Bible as I reassured the paramedic that everything was going to be alright. I could see by the look in his eyes that he was not sure I would make it alive to the hospital.

The next thing I remember was lying on a cold steel table in the x-ray room. The doctors had just informed me that I would be having surgery to repair the severed artery and the broken bone. They would not promise a successful surgery; if too much damage had been done, they would possibly have to amputate my leg. The doctors left the room to inform my friend, my Mom and my brother Ron. My brother's voice would raise and lower obviously strained with concern. I remember my mother sobbing hysterically.

At that moment I prayed, "Lord, if you need my leg, you can have it. But if you don't need my leg, I'd really like to keep it."

In one month of knowing Jesus I did not know much about prayer. However, after I prayed that prayer I felt peace flow over my body. God was in control!

The surgery was successful! A small artery from the top of my right foot had been taken out to repair the damaged one in my leg. My leg was put in a cast to allow the bone time to heal properly. After a ten-day stay in the hospital, I went home for six weeks of recovery.

There is something that would seem very minor to most and yet this was a very significant part of this incident in my life. I was wearing a pair of blue jeans when the accident occurred. As I was being prepped for surgery, my blood-soaked jeans were cut off my body. When I returned home they had been cleaned and neatly repaired. My mother wanted everything to be well with me. Washing and repairing the jeans was what she could do to help bring my life back to a normal state. It puts me in mind of Jesus' Mother, Mary. How difficult it must be for a mother to allow their children the freedom to walk in God's plan.

For the next five years, I had the wonderful opportunity to seek God in prayer and bathe in His Word. I would spend one morning hour and many evenings crying out to God for the souls of my family members and for His perfect will in my life.

He spoke very clearly to me, promising if I would be about His business, He would see to the salvation of my family.

I clung to that promise and moved forward to continue to live my life for Him.

At the end of five years, I received a unique opportunity from the Lord. I felt a call on my life to go to the mission field. I did not know where, when or how, but I felt a strong desire to be on foreign soil. During a Tuesday evening Bible study, conducted in the home of one of our local church members, the pastor's brother-in-law announced the need for a business education teacher to relieve a teacher in Taichung, Taiwan, for a yearlong sabbatical. The missionary, his wife and family were home on leave and desperately looking for someone to take the teacher's place for the teaching year. Over the previous year, God had been dealing with my heart and placing a burden there for mission work. I really did not understand what the Lord meant until I went to the Bible study and felt the tugging in my heart. I responded to the missionary's request and over the next year God continued to prepare my heart while opening doors to make the trip possible.

When it is God's way and His timing, He makes all things possible. I did not have to be approved by a local church or a mission board, nor did I have to raise funds to cover the trip or living expenses for the time I was to be in Taiwan. The school hired me as a "Direct Hire" teacher. I would receive a full salary from the school during my year of teaching. My trip to and from Taiwan was paid for in full by the school. God is a "miracle working" God.

My First Convert

※

I was very young in the Lord and single with all the time in the world at my fingertips. At this time I was living in an old Victorian house in Vinton, Iowa that housed several cozy efficiencies and apartments. My landlady was quite elderly. She was friendly and we visited often while passing in the foyer of the old house. She did not know that I was a Christian.

After what seemed to be two very short years in the old Victorian house, I was preparing to move into a rental home with another friend. I remember the night very clearly, as if I was once again reliving the sacred event. It was a dreary Iowa night in the autumn of the year. The rain sliced at my face and hands as I carried box after box to my waiting car. I had just come back into my efficiency and knelt down to pick up another packed box.

I heard His voice speak ever so clearly, "Go and tell Mrs. M about Me."

I said, "Lord, you mean right now?"

"Yes, right now!" was the definite response from Him.

I quickly got up from the floor and walked rather hesitantly to Mrs. M's apartment door.

I knocked and her small sweet voice responded, "Come, in!"

As I gently pushed the old oak door open there she sat in her overstuffed comfortable chair, as if she had been waiting for me. I fell to my knees at her feet and with no regret began to share my faith in Jesus as my Savior. The Holy Spirit was so very present. As tears streamed down her cheeks, she choked out these words, "I want to know Him too!" She then bowed in prayer and repeated a prayer of acknowledgement of her sin and her need for Jesus to be her Savior. In two to three minutes she had gone from being lost to being totally forgiven. She had found a new Friend – her Savior, Jesus.

This, on my part, was simply an act of obedience. On the Lord's part, it was His perfect timing. He knew Mrs. M's heart and that she was ready to receive Him as her Savior. The Lord had chosen to partner with me that night because He also knew my heart. There was no forethought or blueprint plan on my part. It was a simple response to His request.

Moving On In Him...

༄

It was the summer of 1982. I had returned in late May from Taiwan and settled in once again with my former roommate in Cedar Rapids, Iowa. Debra and I shared a cozy little two-bedroom house in a beautiful part of the city. I began seeking God's wisdom about what He would have for me next. I sought a teaching position in the area and none was to be found.

It seemed as though the entire world had changed drastically though I had only been gone for a year. As I look back, I now know God had done a wonderful work in me. My life was forever changed. I had a new attitude toward and respect for human life – all human life. I could never turn back. It was now only onward and upward in Him.

I met Nancy Jo at a little church in the area. She was working on establishing an organization to fight legal abortions. My friend who sat in the pew next to me had had an abortion several years before. We were seeking God's healing in her life. Nancy Jo was also very familiar with the horror associated with abortion; she had aborted her own Shawna Marie. Nancy Jo, upbeat and outgoing, also sang in a local Christian band. Would I like to come to Des Moines? Perhaps it would be a new beginning. I arrived at Nancy's home in the afternoon. A friend dropped by to visit. It was Nolan. He came to talk. He was so burdened and broken from the strain of the death of his wife who at the age of twenty-three died from a cancer that literally riddled her body. Nolan and Nancy Jo visited in the solarium for sometime. She ministered to him from the Word. Nancy shared about God's love for Nolan.

After our first meeting, Nolan and I began seeing each other. During my visit at Nancy Jo's, I applied for jobs in the area and received a position at a local counseling center. I moved to Des Moines and settled in with Mary Gene, a good friend and a cousin of Doris.

Shortly after I settled in, Nolan and I began to make wedding plans. We were married on October 24, 1982. It was a typical Iowa fall. The leaves were rich in color. We rented a home on 44th Street. It was a new beginning from the Lord. He had plans for us.

Nolan's occupation was full-time pool building and maintenance and part-time sound engineer. We attended the First Assembly of God Church on Merle Hay Road. I had been praying for an opportunity from the Lord for Nolan to use his God-given talent in the audio field. Within the first year of our marriage, the Lord spoke very specifically and gave us two promises. Nolan would run sound before thousands and he would travel from state to state meeting the audio needs of many churches.

All we had was our faith in God that he would work in our lives and use us as His vessels to His glory.

Ronnie Dobbs, from the Jimmy Swaggart Ministries, had made contact with our church looking for an audio engineer. When we heard of the opportunity at the Swaggart Ministries, we felt a gentle, but ever so sure tug on our hearts to respond to what we had heard. Could this be the opportunity I had been praying for? Nolan immediately responded by calling Ronnie Dobbs.

In October of 1984, we left Des Moines for Baton Rouge, Louisiana where we were to embark upon one of the greatest adventures of our life.

The Beginning of a Long Battle

Faith Cometh By Hearing . . .
Romans 10:17
. . . As Told By Nolan

ॐ

I was born on November 13, 1956, in Emporia, Kansas, the fourth and last son of Arlie and Louise Pauley. My parents attended church on a regular basis. At the age of seven, I accepted Jesus as my Savior. The experience was rather vague, but permanent. Once Jesus came into my life, He was the Author and Owner. Looking back on my life, I can see clearly that I belonged to Him. He took control when my life was out of control.

I have always been rather shy and soft-spoken. While growing up, my life was centered around family. My brothers were typical boys, rough and ready to go. If one of us could not come up with a good idea, the other one did.

The year was 1974. At the age of sixteen I was very independent and quite a character. My parents were busy preparing for an extended vacation to Utah to visit relatives. I approached my parents with a "good idea." I pleaded with everything in me. Could I please ride my bike to visit my cousins at their farmhouse? My parent's response was a definite – NO!

The next morning my parents left early for their vacation. I waited quietly in bed until it was clear they were gone and I was free to get my bike and go.

It was March 31st. The cold bleak winter months had officially ended just ten days earlier. In Iowa that did not mean there would not be more wintry days ahead. But for today, the sun was shining, the grass had grown rich and green. The flowers were radiant in color. The Iowa air was particularly fresh. It felt like spring!

My bicycle trip to my cousin's farmhouse would be thirty-five miles, one way, to a small farm community just outside of Des Moines. I left my home in Des Moines at 9:00 A.M. The sun was warm on my face. It was fun riding my bike on the gravel roads going up hill, and the best part, going down hill. I have to admit, I wondered quite often if I was headed in the right direction.

I arrived six hours later to find my aunt hanging

freshly washed clothes in the warm March breeze. There is nothing like the smell of freshly washed clothes that have been dried in the new spring air. My aunt was so happy to see me. My cousins were in town running errands and would be back in two hours.

When my cousins arrived, we hung out, watched television and talked about farming. My cousin had a job the next day with a local farmer. He said he could use some help getting the field ready for spring planting. I agreed to help with whatever I could do for him. I slept soundly that night. There is nothing like the peace and quiet of the country.

We woke early the next morning to the smell of bacon and eggs cooking in the kitchen. My aunt had already been up for an hour before she woke us. This was the custom on the farm. Today was April 1st. It was a cool and dreary day unlike the day before. During the spring the weather can change dramatically in one day. At breakfast we discussed putting dual tires on the tractor for better traction. We then decided changing the tires would take too much time away from our busy day. We finished breakfast and mounted the tractor to go to the field.

My cousin drove, while his girlfriend rode on the left fender of the tractor and I rode on the right fender. As we entered onto the field, we were traveling on an uphill grade. The right wheel of the tractor suddenly hit a deep hole. Without warning, the right fender snapped off the tractor. My body fell directly on the wheel forcing me forward and eventually under the wheel. The wheel ran directly over the midsection of my body. As the wheel rolled over me, I felt what I thought was blood gushing out of my mouth. It was the breakfast I had eaten moments earlier. Dazed and not sure of what had just happened, I immediately went into shock. It would later be determined that my pelvis was broken in three places and my sacroiliac was dislocated.

I was conscious, as time stood still. It appeared as if everything was in slow motion. My cousin ran across the field to call 911. His girlfriend stayed at my side to give whatever comfort she could. The shock of the accident, not to mention the severity of the pain, kept my focus away from the reality of my broken body. The ambulance arrived an hour later and rushed me to the medical center in Des Moines.

Upon arrival at the emergency room, I was given a shot in my left leg to ease the pain. My youth pastor met me at the emergency room and reassured me I was going to be alright. Randy was the kind of guy who got everyone involved in the youth group. He was hardworking and faithful to the group of young people God had put in his care. He was very instrumental in helping me get started running sound in the church for the youth and with the traveling youth singers. Randy was always keen at detecting the abilities and talents of the youth. God had given me a talent to hear the most distinct sounds. This ability was nothing anyone could train to do or develop on his own. The ability, or rather the gift, came directly from the throne room of God. After he realized my interest and abilities with sound, Randy followed through and I began running sound in the main sanctuary for the regular church services. Randy was not only a youth pastor he was a good friend. He was the kind of friend only Jesus could send into a person's life.

My parents were contacted immediately. I was put into traction at the pelvic area and remained in the hospital for two months. My left thigh had been pressed against the soil during the accident. The soil was full of herbicides, which became imbedded into my flesh. My thigh had not been properly cleansed in the emergency room. A staph infection was the result of the injection I was given the day of the accident. It lay dormant for my two-month stay in the hospital.

I was home continuing my recovery time. I walked with a cane to allow more time for my pelvic area to heal properly. The staph infection began to rear its ugly head up in the form of boil like pockets on my thigh. The soft tissue of my thigh looked like honeycomb as Dr. B debrided the area. The debriding process went on for approximately three years. Months at a time I would be in the hospital and then out for short periods of time, until a doctor in Cincinnati, Ohio, developed a serum from the bacteria on my thigh. The serum became the cure for this type of bacterial infection. As the injections were administered the infection was arrested. After four months of outpatient treatment, the infection was gone.

With one simple act of disobedience my life was forever changed. Who would have thought a bike ride to the country would bring such tragedy into my life? I was grateful to God for my restored health. However, there was nothing that could change the circumstances that might not have been. God is always in control. He knew about April 1, 1974 at the beginning of time. My life was engraved upon the palm of His hand and He has known every detail.

My disobedience brought devastating events into my life. An error on the part of the emergency room's staff brought other events that did not have to be. But the Lord was there all the time watching over me and caring for my every need. What the enemy meant for harm God intended for good. The serum had been developed which would help others who would have similar farm accidents. My body was restored back to health. Only scars remain as a gentle reminder of my disobedience. And certainly the lesson learned from the act of disobedience remains fresh in my mind. When the Lord says "no," I wait. When He says "yes," I ask, "When, where and how?"

Psalm 16:8-9

I have set the Lord always before me:
Because, He is at my right hand,
I shall not be moved.
Therefore my heart is glad,
and my glory rejoiceth:
My flesh also shall rest in hope.

৯৭

Knowing that the Lord is always before us has given me great comfort over the years. It is difficult to live our lives for the Lord as we always will receive opposition from the enemy. There are several characteristics of the "wicked," if you will, as described in the first six verses of Psalm 64. The wicked plot in secret and are rebellious in nature. Many times they can be recognized by their bitter words. They have no fear and are drawn to those who are blameless – those living their lives for the Lord. They encourage themselves in what they are doing and are presumptuous to think no one will see their sin. They also convince themselves that their schemes are perfect – no one will know.

God has His answer to those who work iniquity. Suddenly He will deal with them. He will cause them to stumble over their own words and deeds. Their deeds and words will come back to haunt them. The blameless will stand by in awe of God and declare His works. The Lord's works shall be wisely considered and all will learn from them. We will be glad in Him and know that we can trust in Him. All those who are pure in heart will praise and glorify Him.

Daily we are all confronted with the good seed and the bad seed. In the parable of the wheat and tares, the landowner told his servants to allow both the wheat and tares to grow together until the harvest time. At the harvest time the landowner would instruct the reapers to gather the tares first and to bind them in bundles to burn them. Then the wheat would be gathered and put into the barn.

This is our promise from the Lord that He will care for us daily even in the midst of the tares in our lives. He will watch over us as the landlord watched over his fields of wheat. When the enemy came in unaware to the landlord, and the tares were brought to the attention of the landlord, he immediately recognized the source of them. The landlord's response was to allow both to grow together until the harvest. God has allowed both the good seed and the bad seed to grow together. I believe there is a two-fold purpose:

1. This allows us as Christians to grow in our walk with Him.
   a. We will be able to hear Him more clearly.
   b. We will be able to readily recognize when He moves on our behalf.
2. This also allows us as Christians to gain our strength in Him.
   a. As we become weak He becomes strong in us.
   b. In our weakness He is better able to move in our lives and use us as His instruments.

As we set the Lord before us in our daily lives, it becomes more and more difficult for the "tares" to affect our walk with Him. It becomes easier to walk with Him and not be moved by the circumstances that surround us. Our hearts can be glad. Our physical bodies and minds can find rest and renewed hope in Him.

Psalm 64:3 –
The Wicked . . .Their
Tongues – Bitter Words

༄༅

The dream began with a family sitting around what appeared to be the dinner table. One member stood faithfully ready to fulfill any and all requests of the person sitting at the head of the table. All adult members were present with their spouse at their side. The person at the head of the table was talking non-stop. All other members were sitting listlessly. They had already been weakened by the words coming from the mouth of the person at the head of the table. Each word that spewed forth caused those around the table to grow paler in appearance and weaker in their physical condition. Their faces, hands and arms were emaciated. As the words come forth from the head of the table, the other family members were being eaten alive. They were being consumed by the need of the person at the head of the table to be in control at all times; the need to be the center of attention. There appeared to be two things that motivated the person at the head of the table, self and greed. As far as this person was concerned, there was no one but her and no need but her own. Whatever was to happen had to happen for her benefit.

The member who stood ready to serve seemed to be literally sucking in every word spoken, as if it was the gospel truth. I was at the server's side pleading with her not to believe what she was hearing, but to check it out in the Word of God. The server's puzzled look indicated to me she was not in step with the Lord. The server could not discern the truth of the situation and was already deceived. She walked deeper and deeper into the relationship with the person sitting at the head of the table and into the deception.

The person at the head of the table spoke so sweetly to the server, presenting herself as an Angel of Light. Everything from the outward appearance indicated the person at the head of the table belonged to the Lord. The server questioned, "Why are you warning me?" Apparently the server was blind to the condition of the family members sitting around the table.

The family members appeared to be a captive audience. Suspended spiritually, so they were unable to move away from the table to escape the bitter words. The stronghold in the life of the person sitting at the head of the table froze all other family members. The family members were also not able to speak by reason of the stronghold. They could only listen and be emotionally, mentally and spiritually torn apart. This was manifested in their physical bodies. None dare speak or have a differing view than the person sitting at the head of the table.

Over the years it has been one of the easiest things for a "Christian" to say, "I am a Christian. I have accepted Jesus as my Savior." The real question is, "Have we allowed Him to be the Lord of our lives?" And then, "Have we allowed Him to be the Master of our lives?" As we follow through and choose these deeper walks with Him, then we become His servant. We will do whatever He desires and we will go wherever He desires. It is no longer our will, but His.

Shortly after I accepted Jesus as my Savior and Lord, the Lord gave me a very simple but direct command, "Go home, clean out your apartment and give everything you have." As strange as the request was, there was an urgency in my heart to respond to the Lord. I had to give up everything? What could it possibly mean? As I frantically searched my closets, chest of drawers and any boxes I had carefully packed belongings in, it became clear to me what the Lord was referring to. I had many clothes, shoes, accessories and other items that were no longer in use. They were in excellent condition and certainly someone could use them. I proudly took them to the local church. I say proudly, because it was my first personal command from the Lord. I was thrilled to have heard from Him and overjoyed to quickly respond to His request. Pastor Bill's wife came to the door. As I carried armful after armful and box after box of clothing and personal items to the front of the parsonage, Kendra's eyes widened.

Her only response, "Are you sure this is what the Lord would have you do?"

I was sure. One half of the enclosed front porch was now filled with the things the Lord had shown me to give. I felt weight being lifted from my shoulders as peace flooded my soul. It was a simple act of obedience; giving all that I had, letting go of the past and the world. I could have resisted and not responded to the Lord's voice, which would have only opened the door to the enemy through rebellion.

When we call ourselves Christians, but our heart is not totally given to Him, several things can happen:

1. We wrongly influence people by our words or actions. We will be accountable for what we have said or done.
2. We say we are representing the King of Kings and Lord of Lords. We are really only representing ourselves and are living a lie.

3. By wrongly influencing people or by misrepresenting Him, we bring shame on Him. Because of our actions and deeds, many times we keep others who need to receive Jesus as their Savior away from Him.

Who is sitting at the head of your table?

The Nun

꒜

It was the summer of 1984, actually it was July 4, 1984. Nolan had his first hiatal hernia surgery to correct a problem he had with swallowing. Jo was two months old. As I carefully cradled her in my arms we entered the hospital through the main entrance. Immediately in front of us was the elevator that would take us to the floor where Nolan was recovering. As I reached forward to press the button for the floor we needed to go to, the elevator door came open and there stood a four-foot – eleven inch Catholic nun. She was radiant with the joy of the Lord and the presence of God engulfed her. Our eyes met, and our smiles declared a silent greeting one to the other. She stepped forward, with her delicate hands raised as if she was about to praise God.

As she laid her hands upon Jo, she spoke boldly and with confidence, "Blessings upon this child, in the name of Jesus!"

My heart leaped within me and before I could think I responded, "Thank you, Jesus!"

After the nun spoke those words the Holy Spirit (the presence of God) engulfed Jo and me also. As quickly as the little nun appeared, she disappeared. I wanted so much to thank her for being such a blessing to me. I believe she was simply about her Father's business and would accept no glory for herself.

On that particular day, the Lord had chosen to manifest Himself in a direct manner. The nun was His willing vessel and Jo and I were His direct recipients. The nun, through the power of the Holy Spirit, breathed life into Jo and myself. She spoke a blessing for the day and certainly a blessing that would carry over into the years to come.

This experience puts me in mind of a question we all need to ask ourselves. Are we blessing our children or are we cursing our children? Our meeting with the little nun was not by chance. It was a divine meeting ordered by the Lord. That day I learned a valuable lesson. I needed to bless my child in my own personal prayer time, when I spoke directly to her and with her and when I prayed with her. This didn't mean that I had to speak the same words as the nun spoke over Jo, but I needed to carefully choose words of blessing to speak to her. Words that would teach and edify each circumstance or situation that might arise in her life.

Of course, the Scriptures are the words to speak that will teach, but we do not want to bombard our young people with Scripture after Scripture. Our life should be a living testimony; how we handle real life situations or problems should bring clarity to our children about our own personal relationship with the Lord. This should in turn give our children food for thought as to the level of relationship they choose to pursue with the Lord. Speak blessings, pray blessings and be a blessing in the lives of our children. They will, in turn, become a blessing to others and will fulfill a purpose God has for all of us.

Sealed for the Day
of Redemption

ॐ

Jo was born on Friday, May 4, 1984, at 6:02 P.M. She was truly a gift from God, as are all children. She was precious, sweet and delicate at the birth weight of 5 pounds and 13 ounces. Nolan had been told he would never be able to conceive children because his pelvis had been so severely crushed during the tractor accident. However, God had placed his hand of blessing on our marriage early on. Jo's arrival brought with it a new meaning to our lives together. God had seen fit to complete our family. Prior to Jo's birth, I remember vividly crying out to God and promising Him if He would bless us with a child – only one – I would do everything in my power and by His grace to raise our child for Him and to His glory.

We were ordinary people with an extraordinary call upon our lives.

It was a normal Sunday evening after church where we were living in Lakeland, Florida. So we thought. After we arrived home from the Sunday evening service at about 8:30 P.M., we were having our usual nighttime prayer with Jo. She was 3 and 1/2 years old. Nolan asked her if she would like to receive Jesus as her Savior. As Nolan began to pray the most beautiful Holy Spirit inspired prayer, Jo repeated the prayer word for word.

It was one of the most miraculous events I had experienced since my own conversion!

At the end of the prayer, Nolan and I both saw a flash of light – Holy Light – surround and enter into Jo's physical body. She had been sealed for the day of redemption.

Standing on Holy Ground

༈

For the first time, Nolan would be employed full-time in the audio field. What a wonderful opportunity! Nolan traveled overseas on a monthly to bimonthly schedule. The heart of the ministry was to bring the lost to an acceptance of Jesus as their Savior. Then local churches would be established and funded to disciple those who were saved during the crusade meetings.

Though these were difficult times, the joy of being a part of the work of God and having first-hand experience in seeing those who were lost come into the marvelous light of Christ outweighed any discomfort. We were in the battle for the long haul! What we were learning spiritually taught us to stand in the midst of the storm. We were very fortunate to minister with those who shared the same burden for the lost. Nolan's part was the front line work and mine was the "behind the scenes" prayer. We were partners in this adventure, sharing the joy of the victories won for Jesus overseas and in America.

The teachings, preaching and experiences were so deeply imbedded in our hearts, I was thrilled one day to realize the impact. Jo and I were on our way to the store.

Buckled in the car seat looking very serious, she looked up at me and said, "Mama, remember the man that had his face blown off?"

At the age of two, Jo was playing on the floor beneath the pew where we always sat in church. The speaker for that particular Sunday morning happened to be Dave Reever. Many of you know his story. He was in Vietnam fighting in the front lines when he was literally blownup. His face was floating in the water next to him.

That particular sermon so impacted Jo's life that at the age of eight she was sharing her thoughts. Did the man whose face was blown off recover? Yes he did. God restored his health 100%. There were scars, yes but he was restored physically and spiritually became a new creature in Christ.

Early on, Jo saw first-hand what God could and would do in a person's life. She has always had sensitivity for those others might consider undesirable in looks, abilities or lack of wealth.

Experiences like this impacted all three of us to remember God's purpose in our lives.

That would be very important in the years to come.

Holding On to the
Nail Scarred Hand

ॐ

Psalm 142:3

*"When my spirit was over whelmed within
me, Thou didst know my path . . ."*

The evil that surrounded us was overwhelming.
Many of the people were Godly believers who
knew and loved the Lord Jesus and sought Him
daily. Many said they knew and even loved the Lord
Jesus, but their actions and behavior did not reflect
that relationship with Him or a love for Him. And
then there were those who only pretended to know
Him and who spoke vain words of their love for
Him.

We were taking an emotional and mental beating.
It was as if we were being flogged with all the ram-
ifications of such a beating. Which direction would

the torment come from next? We had to walk so carefully because there were so many flavors of Christians. Were we associating with those who really knew Him? Or were the fence riders and pretenders able to deceive us?

One day as I drove from our subdivision that was behind another older and well-established subdivision, I came to the stop sign that marked the end of both. That day became a turning point in the circumstances that surrounded us. Time began to stand still as I sat at the stop sign.

The presence of the Lord filled our vehicle as I began to pray, "Lord, no matter what, we are coming through these circumstances holding on to your nail scarred hands."

As hot tears streamed down my face, I imagined the Lord standing between Nolan and myself. Nolan carried Jo in his free arm. Each of us had our hand in a nail-scarred hand of Jesus. He held our hands firmly as we clung to Him. All I could confess was that we were coming through the circumstances holding on to Jesus, no matter what. Our total focus had to be on Him, because He was the One who would carry us through this trial.

We all need to carefully consider our relationships with others. Are we associating with those who will encourage us in our walk with the Lord? The Lord commands us to love everyone, but He also wants us to walk in His wisdom in our relationships with others. He has to be first in our lives.

Do you have that personal relationship with Him? The kind of relationship where you walk daily with Him? Or are you the one who says you know Him, but your life does not reflect a personal relationship with Him? Or are you simply the pretender?

Daily we need to know Him. Our life needs to reflect a freshness that only time spent with Him can bring.

The Sweet Rose
of Sharon

ॐ

It was spring. God was manifesting Himself in ways we had never experienced. As I walked from the kitchen into our laundry room, I began to smell a sweet, light rose fragrance that had permeated the air. I entered into the garage and the fragrance was stronger there. When I came back into the laundry room my first thought was, " The cap to my laundry freshener must be off the bottle." But, once again, as I entered into the garage I knew it was The Rose of Sharon. The peace of the Lord and the sweet fragrance could not be denied.

I said, "Thank you Lord," not understanding what this was about.

This would also happen at other times. While standing in my bedroom the sweet rose fragrance and the peace of the Lord once again came into the room.

As I stood silent and in awe of God, I allowed the fragrance and peace to enter into my broken spirit.

Up to this point, we had been so inundated with battling the enemy during our prayer time we had no thoughts of asking God to send us His peace and much more His sweet fragrance. I remember sharing this with a good friend and dear sister in the Lord, Lola. We agreed it was a special sign to us from God. But, what was God speaking to us and why?

Unknown to Lola or us, Lola became God's messenger to us from the Brownsville Revival. She had gone to Pensacola after the first of the year in 1997. She told no one and wanted no one to know until she returned. Lola was looking for something more from God. She knew little about the revival, other than she knew she needed to be there. Lola had heard from God.

Upon arrival at the revival, Lola sensed nothing unusual. She sensed the presence of God. Many were prostrate on the floor crying out to God for mercy. She knelt at the altar.

Her first thought was, "Nolan needs to be here."

Lola was very much aware of Nolan's gifting in the audio field. She saw the magnitude of the revival, but more than that, God had spoken to her heart.

Lola's trip to Brownsville was the beginning of our awareness of the revival. The Sweet Rose of Sharon was a sign of His presence in our lives; of what He was going to do for us. It was confirmation in the midst of our six-year battle that He loved us and was moving on our behalf, no matter what circumstances surrounded us.

The six-year battle was like no other circumstance we had ever faced. Every corner we turned confronted us with a new battle within the battle, however God was so faithful to us. He had been with us every step of the way. Many times He simply carried us. Other times He strongly manifested Himself to encourage us and to remind us that His promises are true. He was there all the time. He never left us or forsook us. We belonged to Him through thick and thin. He was teaching us His truths.

Many days our one-on-one relationship with the Lord seemed blurred. But ultimately, He wanted us to know that no matter what circumstances surrounded us, we still and always would belong to Him. Our personal relationships with Him became so precious. If we knew nothing else we knew that He loved us.

Out of the Darkness and Into the Marvelous Light

ॐ

There are times in all of our lives when we walk in places that are spiritually dry or dark. Places we question whether the Lord really opened the door or whether He really sent us there. Did we hear His voice correctly? He spoke ever so softly and certain.

This place for us was a six-year stay at a large church. The pastor was a television evangelist/ preacher that was known all over the United States. He was young, charismatic and very popular. There can be nothing in our lives that replace our personal relationship with the Lord and subsequently our relationship with those God has placed in our lives. This would prove to be the most difficult place to walk that we had yet to encounter and it would not be the last. We had the Lord on our side and we had the experience of ministry work that was sincere and desiring the best for all mankind.

The best we could do during these years was to walk closely with the Lord. Many incidents forced us to lay prostrate before God, seeking Him. It was a very hard place. Many times through the years God refreshed us with the testimony of different members of the church.

Some would say, "The Lord has placed Nolan in this church." They bore witness to his gift and calling. They would pray for strength.

Others would say, "Nolan's life is a sweet fragrance of God's presence, His peace and His steadfastness.

The members saw Nolan's affliction and they saw the strength God had given him to endure. And endure we would, to the very end.

Early one January morning as I woke to the lavender mist sunrise, I quietly spoke, "Nolan are you awake?"

The response was "yes," so I began reminding Nolan of the story of the Israelite's exodus from the land of Egypt. It was the Holy Spirit telling the story through me. He reminded us of the hard labor and the harsh treatment endured by the Israelites. They were waiting for their deliverer. It was a promise to them from God. They would be set free from the bondage and cruelty they had endured for so many generations. They were to pass through the Red Sea to be set free into the land of promise. The land where milk and honey flow. The Israelites were warned by God to stay on the straight and narrow and not to intermingle with the natives of the land. They would then be blessed.

God, Himself, by the power of the Holy Spirit, was speaking to us ever so gently about a coming change in our life. We were thrilled to have heard from Him. Our prayers were being answered and God was beginning to let us in on His next set of plans for our life. Where was the land of Canaan? How would we get there and when would we be going? As the winter faded into spring, we received a phone call from Brownsville Assembly of God in Pensacola, Florida. They were looking for an experienced audio engineer/technician. Nolan was recommended for the position by a previous supervisor from another ministry.

By this time, Nolan had been accustomed to running sound in churches with seating capacities of 5,500 or more.

Nolan questioned, "Why would Rick recommend me to a church that only seats 2,500 people?"

It seemed strange to us and yet Nolan pursued this open door. Within the next two weeks, the church flew Nolan to Pensacola to interview.

After attending the weekend evening services, Nolan called home with the good news, "You will not believe this Jan! This church is in the throes of a move of God like has never been seen in our time."

After talking to the person who would be his immediate supervisor, Nolan flew home revived and refreshed from the touch of God he had received. He had renewed hope. God had seen our tears and heard our cries. Nolan was certain God was moving on our behalf.

We would wait to hear from Brownsville. They were to have a board meeting to make a final decision. Days, a week and then another month went by without a word from Pensacola. It was like an eternity to us. The battle where we were continued to escalate, just like it had for the Israelites in the land of Egypt. We felt like we were living the Word of God, frantically gathering our few possessions to leave for the Promised Land.

Brownsville Assembly of God was in the initial stages of revival and they were inundated with people, revival services and the media. We would later come to learn that because of the move of God there was little time for anything else. With all the necessary people present at night, even a board meeting became almost impossible. However, we were about to embark upon a most awesome move of God.

We waited expectantly, but received no phone call. Jo's spring break from school was just around the corner. Nolan wanted Jo and I to see what was going on at Brownsville? We prayed and decided the only thing to do was to go. Since the initial phone call, we were sensing a growing attachment to a church we had never been to, to people we had never met and to a place we knew nothing about. Was this the Lord making a change in us?

In mid March of 1997 we left on vacation to Pensacola, Florida, destination Brownsville Assembly of God. Thirteen hours later we arrived in Pensacola. We were cautiously excited not knowing what to expect. Jo had invited a friend to vacation with us. They immediately fell in love with the beach. As we settled into our hotel room, Nolan made arrangements to attend more of the revival services. We would be in Pensacola for the weekend and then on to Baton Rouge, Louisiana, to visit our good friends Johnny and Lynn.

Nolan attended the services on Friday and Saturday evenings and we all went to church Sunday morning. It was Easter Sunday. What a beautiful way to celebrate! We were relaxed and at peace with the possibility of a new ministry opportunity and we were able to see our friends once again. After service we drove to Baton Rouge to spend the next few days. We continued to relax and enjoy our time away from home. However, Nolan was determined to get a final answer from Brownsville regarding their need for audio personnel.

While returning from Baton Rouge, Nolan decided we would go to the main office at Brownsville to see Pastor Carey. It was Friday morning, the final day we would be in Pensacola before returning home. We arrived at the office and checked in with the secretary. Nolan asked if I would wait in the office area while he went to the church to find Bennie. As Pastor Carey became available, Nolan and Bennie stepped into the office building. As we merged together in the lobby of the main office, it became clear that Pastor Carey and Bennie both thought the other was taking care of the details of hiring Nolan. It was agreed Pastor Carey would contact Pastor Kilpatrick to arrange a board meeting. Pastor Carey escorted us back to the church for a brief tour and introduction to other employees. As we walked down the hall to the television department the Holy Spirit swept over us. It was a burst of energy and confirmation we were to be at Brownsville.

A special board meeting was called for that evening at 6:00 P.M. Nolan was approved as a new employee. Exhausted as we were, we got into our car and started home.

Our exodus in many ways paralleled the exodus of the Israelites. The Israelites were considered property or a possession of the Egyptians. They would not be allowed to leave Egypt without contention. The Egyptians believed they had full control over the Israelites and would make all necessary decisions regarding them. Not so! The Lord was in control and had other plans, just as the Lord had other plans for us. It was God's call – not man's call.

On April 18, 1997, Nolan began his employment at Brownsville Assembly of God. When we first moved to Pensacola, the enemy, once again, fought hard. But the Lord carried us through.

On November 1, 1997, Nolan became the Apogee dealer for this region of the country. In the previous places where we lived, the Apogee dealership had always taken by someone else. Nolan always said he would love to secure this dealership somewhere. It was his secret heart's desire. That was exactly what the Lord had in mind when He called us to Pensacola. This was the Lord's answer to an eighteen-year long prayer. We wanted to do more for Him. He was giving us the open door.

The next few months and years were quality times in the Lord. Never could we have foreseen or anticipated what was about to happen next. The Lord was sheltering us from the impending storm.

Multitudes In Prayer
Phase I – Phase XI

৯৯

MULTITUDES IN PRAYER – PHASE I

On August 30, 2000 Nolan went into Baptist Hospital for what was to be a fairly routine hiatal hernia surgery. On August 31st he was cheerfully receiving visitors in his room. The surgery had gone well, but Dr. C felt the recovery was not normal, so he called in a kidney specialist. The kidney specialist came to see Nolan mid-afternoon on August 31st. He told Nolan he was waiting for a bed to open up in SICU so he could be "aggressive" and give Nolan further tests. At that point no one knew what would be found. That afternoon at 5:30 P.M., Nolan was transferred from a regular room to a bed in CCU because there was no bed available in SICU. I remember this well. As the nurses came to transfer Nolan to CCU he was talking to me on the phone. He was happy, excited and relieved the surgery was over.

MULTITUDES IN PRAYER – PHASE II

At 8:30 A.M. on Friday, September 1, 2000, I arrived in CCU. Nolan was barely aware of who he was not to mention where he was. Prior to my arrival Nolan was flipping from the head of the bed to the end as if he were a fish out of water. The pain he was experiencing was beyond what any human could endure. By 9:30 A.M., I was asked to wait outside Nolan's room.

Nolan's nurse Tiffany spoke softly, "Nolan could possibly code."

Nolan had gone into respiratory arrest. The team of nurses paralyzed him mentally and physically with special medications to allow them to put him on a ventilator. By 4:00 P.M. Nolan's blood pressure bottomed out. His body was going into a state of shock. He was given dopamine to keep his blood pressure stable. Jo and I were called back to the hospital. I remember feeling like I was under the influence of a body size shot of novocaine. It was as if horse blinders had been placed on my eyes so that I did not look to the left or the right, but only straight ahead. Brother John, Pastor Gary and Mary were my three faithful friends. Brother John was directing me forward.

While Pastor Gary was always confident – "He's going to take up his bed and walk." And dear Mary – my friend and sister in the Lord – who also happened to be a nurse, was a shelter in the midst of the storm. Mary interpreted each report every step of the way. At this time Dr. C had no conclusive evidence to confirm what was going on in Nolan's body.

This was the first time Jo had seen her father in this condition. I had not mentioned it hoping it would not be necessary. I was waiting to decide how I would explain it to her and where we would find the Lord in all of this. I had no choice now. As Jo entered into her father's room the look on her face expressed shock, disbelief and overwhelming fear. She had never seen another person in this frozen state in her short 16 years of life. She thought her father was going to die.

Jo leaned over her father with tears streaming down her cheeks and said, "Dad please fight. You have to get better. You have to come to my graduation and walk me down the isle when I get married."

God would not allow me to think anything. I was there as His vessel.

MULTITUDES IN PRAYER – PHASE III

The following morning I received a 4:00 A.M. phone call from John, Nolan's attending nurse. Nolan had spiked a fever of 108 degrees. We were once again called to come to the hospital. When we arrived, Nolan was covered from head to toe with cooling blankets and ice packs. His kidneys had failed and it was now determined by blood work that Nolan had sepsis, a very fatal infection in the blood stream. The nurses prepared Nolan for dialysis by placing hemo dialysis catheters in his body. Later in the morning, as the fever steadily dropped, Nolan stabilized and seemed to be responding to our voices. Mary, once again, was right at my side talking to Nolan. She teasingly told him if he would get well the front stage singers would never give him a problem again. He smiled twice at Mary. We were elated. Sunday, September 3rd was more of the same positive responses. The Lord was so very present. All I could feel was His peace. I had no thoughts of the outcome; I only knew that God was very present.

We had to wait to see where Nolan was neurologically because of the high fever. Kathy spent Sunday evening through 6:00 A.M. Monday morning with Nolan – waiting and praying. She was the "watchman on the wall," keeping a vigil not only for Nolan but, for the nurses, doctors and other technical support staff.

This I know, God graced John to hold the reigns of care for Nolan's life that night. He was bold and aggressive in the care he gave Nolan and yet a very humble and God fearing man.

As John sat at the table next to Nolan's bed, monitoring his stats, he looked up at Jo and me and simply said, "It's in God's hands now."

MULTITUDES IN PRAYER – PHASE IV

On Saturday, September 2, 2000 my mother and sister Mary arrived in Mobile on a Delta flight from

Cedar Rapids, Iowa. My dear friend Lynn, of 15 years had driven in from Baton Rouge, Louisiana on Friday, September 1st. I really could not have walked through this time without them. Hindsight tells me they were more aware of the seriousness of Nolan's condition. And yet I have to believe it was God protecting me emotionally and mentally.

By Monday, September 4th, it became clear to Dr. C that Nolan had pancreatitis along with the sepsis that had set in. It was a matter of large doses of antibiotics – the most powerful ones – and waiting. Waiting for God to move. The peace in Nolan's room was undeniable. The brokenness of Nolan's co-workers and friends was encouraging. They were with me in this and they were praying. Praying without ceasing. Lynn quietly slipped away to grieve. She was heartbroken to see Nolan in this condition.

Sometime during the Labor Day weekend, Pastor Gary took me aside and privately asked if there was any question in my mind about Nolan's eternal status. I said there was no doubt. I knew if Nolan died at any moment, he would enter the gates of heaven and the Lord would say, "Well done my good and faithful servant." Pastor Gary then shared a story about how he had prayed for Nolan on Sunday during the prayer time. Nolan then turned and prayed for Pastor Gary. Pastor Gary said it was undeniable. The power of the Holy Spirit fell. As Nolan prayed, Gary received a touched from God.

The week in many ways was uneventful. We considered it a major victory when Nolan was taken off the dopamine. It was a sign that his condition was stabilizing. I took any little positive change and thanked God for it. By this time Nolan's abdomen was extended and his legs, arms, hands and face were extremely swollen. When we would talk to him and ask him to blink his eyes if he could hear us, it was a delayed reaction, but he always blinked. Conscious or not, I believed he was with us. He remained stable through the 11th day of September.

Carole and Lorie, two of the worship team singers, came at night and sang hymns of praise to God to bring comfort and peace to Nolan. As they stood next to his bed and sang, God's presence filled the room. Later I was to learn they had come two or three other times to sing to Nolan. They were bearing the burden of his illness in love. God is so good.

MULTITUDES IN PRAYER – PHASE V

On Tuesday, September 12, 2000, Janet one of the night nurses, called at 3:30 A.M. Clear fluid was gushing out from the top of Nolan's incision. It progressively became pus. The good part about this situation was that it was coming out rather than remaining in his body to create more problems. Radiology came that day to take Nolan for an x-ray and cat scan of his chest. He was being prepared for exploratory surgery to see why there was pus oozing from his incision. The surgery was to be performed at 7:30 that evening. At this point, Dr. C really did not have any hope for Nolan's recovery. Nolan was like a lying dead man and Dr. C was like a walking dead man. The compassion that flowed from Dr. C was incredible.

I remember he looked me directly in the eye and said, "I am sorry. I haven't an answer for what has happened."

That was "OK", because I knew God did have the answer. All I could do was look back at him and nod my head in a way that indicated no fault.

The surgical waiting room was crowded that night with friends, co-workers and those we maybe did not know very well. Everyone there was and had been pulling in the same direction in prayer. We were asking God for a miracle. A miracle that I now realize went far beyond any human comprehension. A miracle only God could perform. The Lord had totally consumed Nolan's life and had every detail of Nolan's healing in His care and control.

It seemed as though when January 1, 2000 came, Nolan was simply not well. I have to say his health over the previous 17 years of our marriage had not been good. We made numerous trips to the local emergency centers for a variety of conditions ranging from bowl obstructions to pain in the chest. In the past four years, Nolan was taking high blood pressure medicine, medicine to control his cholesterol level and different medicines to control the major acid build up in his stomach.

As the year 2000 progressed, I began to seek the

Lord for a complete healing for Nolan, "Lord, heal his body from head to toe, inside and out; heal Nolan's soul, mind and spirit. We need a complete healing."

My prayers continued, "Lord it's time for Nolan to walk in good health so he may continue and complete the work You have set before him."

I had prayed many times over the years healing for Nolan. He has always been so broken physically. When we are in poor health, it affects both our mental and emotional condition, not to mention our spirits and souls. I was asking God to restore Nolan to the person He wants all of us to be – a whole person.

As the year unfolded, we made five trips to the emergency center at Baptist Hospital. During one of those visits Nolan was admitted to the hospital and a heart catheter was placed in his heart. Blockage was found in the artery behind his heart. That morning a stint was placed in that artery. A day later he went home with a prescription for high blood pressure medicine that was one half of the original dose he had been taking. I thought his physical problems were on the mend.

As I said earlier, the surgical waiting room was full to overflowing with believers expecting a miracle from God. The surgical team had already taken Nolan to the surgery room. The team was very tender and compassionate toward me. All the necessary information was given. I signed a release form for the anasteseologist, and the head surgical nurse asked if I had any questions. I said no.

The surgery did not take long. Dr. C stood at the waiting room door while my friend Mary gathered up Jo and me. We walked across the hall into a smaller waiting room to hear the news.

Dr. C began with, "The surgery went well."

A massive abscess had been found. It began at the pancreas and grew behind the stomach and came to the front of the stomach area. It had spread throughout the abdominal cavity. Dr. C was able to completely remove the abscess and clean the abdominal cavity. However, it was necessary to leave the incision open, but covered with a plastic wrap. Drains were placed in three different locations in the abdominal cavity to rid Nolan's body of the infection. This was a major victory. Dr. C was positive for the first time regarding Nolan's condition. The waiting room crowd went wild with praises to God when Mary shared Dr. C's findings. Relief overwhelmed me.

MULTITUDES IN PRAYER – PHASE VI

The next day, Dr. F ordered dialysis. It would be a four-hour process. The dialysis would filter out any impurities and help relieve Nolan of any excess fluids. He was still very extended. Dr. F reassured me in a very compassionate manner. He looked me right in the eye and very peacefully told me Nolan's kidneys were going to function normally. Dialysis was simply a necessary procedure to help Nolan recover. Later that afternoon, dialysis began. I met Priscilla,

the dialysis specialist. She was an extremely delight-
ful person. She was born again and full of God. We
talked about Jesus, His healing power and what God
was doing and what He was going to do for Nolan.
We shared daily devotionals. I have to admit all of
the nurses, technicians and support staff were such a
blessing to me. All exhibited their faith in different
ways. It was precious to me. Jo was strengthened by
their steady forward progress. They faithfully
answered every question. They were so good to
explain Nolan's progress to Jo. We were treated with
the utmost respect. From the time Nolan was
intibated to the day he first spoke seemed like an
eternity. God was there all the time.

Dr. C had discovered blood clots in Nolan's legs.
When the time came to close Nolan's incision, Dr. C
would place filters in the main artery of each leg.
This would keep the blood clots from reaching the
lungs. Dr. C was certain about one thing, between
today and when he would close the incision, if a
blood clot moved into the lungs, then that is the way
it was meant to be. The incision would hopefully be
closed in two to three days. There had been steady
improvement over the last twenty-four hours.
Nolan's neurological status was still uncertain.
However, he had been heavily sedated to keep him
from fighting the ventilator tube. It was impossible
to know Nolan's final condition at this time.

The next two days were days of waiting. Prayer
continued to bombard the gates of Heaven. We'll

never know who and how many prayed. It was a ripple effect – this person who knew this person who knew this person. Person after person, city after city, state after state and international prayers went out for Nolan. The swelling in Nolan's face, hands, arms, legs and feet had gone down to normal. The dialysis and prayer worked. Surgery to close the incision was scheduled for 8:00 A.M. Saturday, September 16th. I was excited and relieved. Progress was being made. God was answering prayer. I could see Dr. C regaining his confidence.

Early Saturday morning Brother John and my good friend Jean and daughter Brittany joined Jo and me for the surgery. Everyone was prayed up, Dr. C was ready for the surgery and the 8:00 A.M. hour had arrived. Dr. C would be exploring for any more abscesses. He would install the filters in the leg arteries and perform a tracheotomy for the ventilator tube. The incision would then be closed. Today was another Victory in Jesus! This would be Dr. C's second positive report. There were no more abscesses. The tracheotomy procedure went quickly and the inside wall of the incision was closed along with the outside flesh.

MULTITUDES IN PRAYER – PHASE VII

Nolan was stable and responsive on Sunday. Once again, he would blink if I would ask him to. At this point it was still thought by the medical staff that his response was involuntary. On Monday night and early Tuesday morning, Nolan spiked another fever. This time it was 103 degrees. The cooling blanket and ice packs were placed on Nolan. Dr. Q, the infectious disease doctor, found a fungal infection in one of the September 5th cultures. This was not good. On Wednesday, September 20th, Nolan's blood pressure once again dropped dramatically. A dopamine drip was restarted to stabilize his blood pressure. He was once again non-responsive. Dr. W, the lung specialist, reported that Nolan's lungs were not doing as well as they had been the two previous days.

One ray of hope for this day, the sedation medicine Nolan had been getting was dropped to one half the original amount. A small, but very important victory! It was possible that surgery would have to be performed to open the incision to continue to help keep the abdominal cavity drained. Jo and her friends Jenn and Kristi visited Nolan. Kristi brought three roses – one for each of us.

I arrived early on Thursday, September 21st to meet with Moses, a new night nurse. Moses had called the previous evening to report Nolan had been raising his hands in praise to God. Nolan moved his arm across his chest just like he would at home to get more comfortable. That was encouraging. It was an indication Nolan was coming back to reality. He lifted his head from the pillow as if he wanted to get up. He opened his eyes, blinked and opened and closed his mouth. We were all thrilled. It was what appeared to be deliberate movement.

Dr. Q was considering a fungal antibiotic on an every other day basis. This would be added to what Nolan was already being given. Dr. F reported his blood pressure and kidneys as marginal. He would possibly order pre-dialysis in the next few days.

On the September 22nd morning CT Scan Dr. C found nothing significant. No new abscess growths. Another drain was inserted today to begin the pre-dialysis. Nolan had begun again to swell in his hands, arms, feet and legs. The pre-dialysis was to begin at 4:30 that afternoon. It would be a slower process so as not to affect Nolan's blood pressure or other vital signs. The fluid was being removed to help his kidneys function normally. It was unnerving to see Nolan attached to the pre-dialysis machine. The machine would slowly pull blood from Nolan's body, cleanse it in the machine's filter and then slowly return the blood through another tube. It was another moment of complete faith in the Lord.

God always has divine appointments for us. That night I went back to CCU. I was concerned. David, the night nurse posed a very interesting question, "Are we prolonging life or prolonging death."

David then began to explain the code system: Code one, two and three. Code one means to do everything in the nurse's power to assist Nolan; Code two – do only certain designated procedures; and Code 3 – do nothing and wait. The thought of making any kind of decision was overwhelming; much more because such a decision regarding

Nolan's life would not leave room for God. No, there would be no decision other than to wait upon Him. What the devil means for harm God intends for our good.

I was able to speak with Dr. F the next day about Nolan's chances of survival. The bowel perforations were a surgical problem; the worst he had ever seen in his fifteen years of practice. He gave Nolan a 20% chance to live. Only one in five would survive this type of problem. Johnny and Seth, the Ward family and Mary and Dean visited today. They were a joy and encouragement to us. It was a time of mental and emotional rest for Jo and me when visitors came. We knew others were carrying the burden with us, but many times for us. God is so faithful to send those who are equipped for the job.

Nolan was tolerating the pre-dialysis very well. Nolan's tolerance for all the procedures was the biggest part of the battle. God was giving His grace to Nolan's body. Four hundred cc's of fluid were drained. Two times the amount they had hoped would drain. Moses was excited and so was I. It was always so good to hear those positive reports. I took each and every one as an indicator from the Lord. Somehow this would all pass. God's promises had not been completely fulfilled in our lives. His work for Nolan was not yet complete.

Today was Sunday, September 24th. Around 9:30 A.M., my friend Mary, the other Mary, stopped at our house to visit. I could feel God's strength coming from her. I am sure she wasn't aware of how God was using her. That is the beauty of how He works – so abundantly and completely. He never leaves any need unmet. It was good to sit and visit over a cup of coffee. Henry David Thoreau once wrote, "My friend shall forever be my friend, and reflect a ray of God to me." That was Mary, a friend forever reflecting a ray of God to me.

Dr. E saw Nolan on Sundays. He was a partner with Dr. Q. They would start a fourteen-day series of fungal infection treatment. Depending on the outcome after fourteen days another series of nine days would possibly be needed. The antibiotics were the strongest given. The dopamine was decreased to five milligrams to help the kidneys function better. Jo, Mr. John, the Ward family, Steve and our neighbors, Jerry and Carol visited. Mary called to see how we were doing.

I woke up early the next morning and called Moses to see how the night had gone. Nolan appeared to have jaundice in his eyes. He had not been very responsive throughout the night. I arrived at the hospital at 9:15 A.M. Nolan blinked when I asked if he could hear me. He seemed to feel pain in his incision area. Dr. Q would start cultures today to see if the antibiotics were arresting the fungal infection. She would watch the cultures for five days. I finally was able to see Dr. C after what seemed to be a very long weekend. I shared with him what the night nurse had told me.

I asked, "Are we prolonging life or prolonging death?"

From where we stood outside Nolan's room Dr. C very thoughtfully looked in at Nolan and said, "We're moving forward!" His response was very definitive.

Today, Nolan had the hiccups. Gio, the respiratory technician, suctioned clear fluids from Nolan's lungs. That was a good sign.

MULTITUDES IN PRAYER – VIII

Tuesday, September 26, 2000 marked the end of the fourth week of Nolan's stay in the hospital. Dr. C was in early that morning and told the nurse, Kay that Nolan would recover. Kay shared with me later that day. A wonderful Christian woman seeing God answering our prayers was excited. Kay also said Nolan would recover. Everyone was pulling for Nolan. It was as if he was on one end of a rope and all those in prayer were on the other end. We were pulling him through a small enclosure like a tunnel. Slowly but surely he was being inched through to our side.

In the night Nolan had spiked a fever of 102 degrees. Moses was able to get it under control with Tylenol. His temperature was back to normal by the time Kay arrived. Fevers many times are a good thing. If Nolan had a reasonable fever, no higher than 102 degrees, then the infection was possibly being fought off. The pre-dialysis was going well.

Priscilla brought in extra copies of my month-by-month, day-by-day devotionals. She had borrowed the originals to make copies for herself and others wanting something to guide them each day. Kay borrowed some of our CD's. She was hungry for worship music. We were all growing in our faith in God in different ways. The beauty in watching God move in all of our lives' was breath-taking. He was painting a beautiful picture on canvas to capture these moments in time. It would be hung in the halls of eternity for all of heaven's courts to gaze upon its beauty.

Wednesday was not a good day. Nolan's arms were stiff and his hands curled in an unnatural posture. Dr. C called in a neurologist and a MRI was scheduled for the next day. Little did we know it would be a miraculous day!

On Thursday, September 28th, Nolan was taken early in the morning for the MRI. It appeared to the attending nurse, Linda that Nolan was agitated. He was in the machine from his shoulders up, but was not happy with the procedure. He was twisting and turning as if to free himself from the machine.

Linda called, "Nolan!"

And Nolan said, "What?"

Linda and Gio were startled. Did she hear what she thought she heard? Gio confirmed. He also heard Nolan speak. Linda called Nolan's name again.

Nolan responded, "What?" once more.

Linda proceeded, "Are you in pain?"

Nolan nodded his head and said, "Yes."

Just to make sure Linda once again called, "Nolan!"

His response was again, "What!"

Linda was certain Nolan's responses were cognitive responses. I arrived at 11:00 A.M. that morning and was greeted by the staff. They were ecstatic at what had taken place. It certainly was rapturous delight. They had been waiting all morning to tell me the good news. I was overwhelmed with their joy and sense of accomplishment. We certainly were moving forward.

Later that day Linda called for Nolan. He stuck his tongue out at her. She asked him if he was mad at her and he said, "No!"

Dawn also called his name and he responded with, what?

Pastor Bill and the Reverend Jodi visited. Nolan responded to their voices by moving his head and arms, lifting his head from the pillow in a vague attempt to get up. He had excellent color in his face and the morning EEG indicated there was brain activity. We were still waiting for the MRI results.

My brother Ron flew into Mobile on Friday, September 29th. On our way back to the hospital Ron was sharing his thoughts in hopes he would ease the shock of what he believed was going to happen. Ron believed there was no medical reason for recovery. That was very true. However, there was a possible Divine reason.

When we arrived at the hospital, Nolan was responding to questions with "what" and "no." He was also shaking his head in a yes – no fashion when asked certain questions. Dr. C ordered pre-therapy and was in the process of deciding what food to give him. The Radiologist's report came back negative on the MRI. Well, not totally negative. Nolan had a case of sinusitis.

Saturday, September 30th, was a beautiful day. It was eighty-five degrees with little humidity. Nolan was very tired and was resting peacefully. His temperature ranged from 99.6 – 100.6 degrees. During the previous night there had been seepage from the intestines through the incision. On Friday three drains were removed from the incision. This seepage through the incision was a good thing. It was not remaining inside Nolan's body to create more problems. It was necessary to change Nolan's bandage often during the night.

Elvira, a mobilization technician, began the daily exercise routine with the stretching and pulling of muscles. Dr. F, the neurologist, was putting pressure on various points of Nolan's fingernails.

Nolan spoke very clearly, "Don't do that!"

Nolan's voice was small but very definite. He felt the pain and was able to respond in a clear manner.

I was privileged to a first hand look at the radiologist's report. The report read exactly as was told by the doctor and nurses. The person who allowed me to see the report did so because I would then be able to refute any talk to the contrary. It was simply nothing other than a miracle from God. It was His keeping power, His staying hand and in Nolan's situation, His perfect will.

MULTITUDES IN PRAYER – PHASE IX

Now would begin the process of weaning Nolan from the various medications to be able to wake him up. He had been weaned from the ativan drip on September 28, 2000. His blood pressure since then had been high. The nurses decided to continue the ativan by injection every four hours. Ativan is the type of medication used to help people reorient themselves to their surroundings. It is especially useful for a patient that has an extended stay in the hospital.

On October 1st, Dr. W weaned Nolan from the ventilator for approximately three hours. He did very well on his own. This would be a process over days because the doctors did not want to cause Nolan to work harder than was necessary.

Dawn was the day nurse and Jeff was the night nurse. Dawn and I shared a great deal about our past lives and about the wonderful things God was doing in our lives. We talked a great deal about personal relationships and how to handle situations in a Godly fashion. We were there for each other. The nurses made my days brighter. I can only hope I lightened their load somewhat. Jeff reported Nolan had slept with His eyes closed. This was the first in days.

When I spoke with Jeff over the phone he said, "We're just hanging out."

The more real and transparent I was with the nurses the more real and transparent they were with me. Along with their work, each nurse had his or her own personal burdens to bear. There were many times we laughed over the silliest things, especially when Nolan began to wake up. I had warned them that their job might be more difficult when Nolan woke up. His first reaction would be to get out of the hospital.

Monday, October 3, Nolan was off the ventilator 8 hours and doing very well. The ativan was increased to every two hours. On Tuesday, Nolan was responding with yes, no or a shake of his head. He was off the ventilator for nine and one half-hours with no ativan until 2:30 P.M. He was given liquid food through the tube in his nose that ran directly to his stomach. Progress was being made. Nolan was becoming more aware and more confident he was ready to leave the hospital.

As of Wednesday, October 4th, there was nothing growing on the cultures regarding any further infections. Nolan remained on the ventilator, continued the ativan every four hours and was given Reglan to help the food that was in his stomach move through his intestines.

The next day would prove to be a very interesting day. At Dawn's command, Nolan squeezed both of her hands, wiggled both set of his toes and blinked both of his eyes. Dawn then asked Nolan to put one finger up and wave his hand.

Nolan stuck his tongue out and said, "No," with a puzzled look that said why are you asking me to do these things?

And he promptly said, "Would you be quiet!"

Teresa, the vent tech, jokingly asked, "Is she bothering you?"

Nolan responded with a roll of his eyes and a smile. That's Nolan! He loves to tease. As Dawn shared the morning's events, we laughed until our sides hurt. All the nurses were so excited about any communication with Nolan. There was never any offense taken on the nurses' part. They were thrilled he was thinking and talking. Linda was right – Nolan's responses were cognitive. He had to think them through.

As I walked into the room, Nolan stretched his arms out to hug me. I leaned over and told Nolan I was there for the day. He focused his eyes directly on me for the first time and shook his head yes and smiled. He was very much aware and looking directly at me.

I asked, "Are you in pain?" He shook his head, no.

A hold was put on the liquid food. It may have been too soon for his digestive system. His breathing was more normal and his kidney levels were heading into the normal range. So many positive signs! Nolan was more calm and aware. He focused his eyes on me a second time and winked when I told him everything was going to be alright. We listened to a Rita

Springer compact disk together. It was a wonderful time of complete peace.

On Friday, October 6th, Nolan was tired but responding well. Brother John, Johnny and Brenda came to visit. When Brenda walked into the room Nolan stretched forth his arms to embrace her with a hello hug. He was recognizing everyone. There was no loss of memory, only a loss of a little time. Nolan was off the vent for twelve consecutive hours. He was gaining stamina. The next three days were much of the same. They were good days with rest and peace. Dr. C announced how pleased he was at Nolan's progress.

He looked at me with his usual look, "Nolan will get up and walk out of here."

It was so good to hear the positive reports.

When Dr. Q arrived she smiled and said to Nolan, "I have been praying for you – plus three thousand other people and I'm sure more." She laughed at the possibility of the number of people praying for Nolan. The number of people praying for one person was beyond anyone's comprehension. Every day Dr. Q would tell me she was praying for us. She would remind me to hold on to my faith. God's ways are higher than our ways and He has all the necessary connections.

Priscilla and Kay stopped in to see how Nolan was doing. They were in different departments but took time from their work to let me know they were still thinking of me and praying for us. God was stretching all of us in our faith. Many were by-standers watching the miracle unfold.

Nolan spoke very clearly to Margie and me, "I want to go home."

There was special prayer for the perforations in Nolan's intestines. They were caused from the abscess. Pastor Gary faithfully sent e-mail every morning to the entire staff at Brownsville Assembly of God. They were praying without ceasing. Many times a group would stop in the middle of the hallway of their offices and pray for Nolan. One weekend in particular there was the men's prayer retreat. Pastor Bill felt the group should stop what they were doing and pray for Nolan. All the men stopped, knelt on the floor and began interceding. That prayer sustained Nolan and brought about many changes over the next few days.

MULTITUDES IN PRAYER – PHASE X

Tuesday, October 10, 2000, was another victory day. The liquid food Nolan had been given began going through his intestines. His system woke up and was digesting the food. This would be another major turning point for Nolan's recovery. Margie, the day nurse, was changing Nolan's bandage that covered the incision.

Nolan looked up at her and said, "I'm mad at you."

Nolan had determined very quickly that Margie was more of a soft touch. It would not take much to get her to give him Cokes and whatever extra goodies he wanted. Margie was the sweetest, kindest person you would ever want to meet. She was extremely efficient in her work and obviously had a soft spot in her heart for her patients.

October 11th was the beginning of the seventh week of stay in the hospital. Nolan was tolerating the food well. He had no assistance from the vent today and he was off for eleven hours. Nolan was resting well, he was peaceful and his heart rate and blood pressure were excellent. He had food through the tube to his stomach for forty-eight hours. Pastor Gary, Randy, Johnny and Kara visited. It was another "Thank you Jesus!" day.

Pastor Richard, the Reverend Jodi and Pastor Bill visited about mid-morning on Thursday. Nolan cried when he saw them. Another realization of where he was and who his friends are. Nolan managed to talk Margie into allowing his hands to be untied. It had been necessary to restrain his hands. He could not attempt to get up because his muscles were not yet strong enough. As I said earlier Nolan would take any opportunity he had to get out of the hospital. At this point, he had no clue as to what he had been through. It wasn't time to tell him. As far as he knew he was perfectly capable of getting out of bed on his own. NOT!

Nolan was currently receiving only a small dosage of morphine during the dressing changes. Dr. W cut the dosage of ativan in half and only as needed. I was very relieved. Nolan had been obviously having nightmares. It was evident from the expressions on his face. While these medications control pain and help acclimate patients to their surroundings, they have obvious negative side effects.

Christy, the occupational therapist, and James her partner in therapy, began their work on October 9th, with immediate positive results. Christy noticed what great upper and lower arm movement Nolan had. He was lying more on his right side now, which indicated he could at least move in the bed on his own. They were working with Nolan to get him to sit at the edge of the bed and balance on his own. They would also place him on a flat bed that positioned into a chair.

One of the high points during this time was when Dr. C stopped in Mary's office at Sacred Heart Hospital.

With a big smile Dr. C proudly announced, "Miracles happen every day." He went on about his business. In every way, people were being drawn together. Because of Nolan's illness, there was a new camaraderie and respect between co-workers. God was weaving His way into the hearts and minds of staff members, co-workers and friends. He was making Himself known in a fresh and new way. The nurses in CCU told me on more than one occasion that Dr. C told them what a good job they had done and were doing. Dr. C's show of appreciation for their hard work meant more to them than anything.

It brought the staff to a new level of respect for the doctors. It was the beginning signs of a job well done. God was constantly working behind the scenes.

Janet was on during the night shift. She came in to greet Nolan.

"I'm here to take care of you this evening."

Nolan responded with a blow of a kiss with his hand.

The next morning Janet called at 7:00 A.M. Nolan had loosed his hands from the tie restraints. He pulled the food tube out of his nose and removed the bandage from his incision.

Nolan had meant what he said two days earlier, "I'm hungry. I want some food."

Dr. C popped in ten minutes later and ordered soft foods by mouth. His incision was OK and his hands were restrained again. The main concern was that he would try to get out of bed. Later that morning Nolan ate Jell-O, chicken broth, apple juice and Italian Ice. It tasted soooooooooooooooo good. This was his first bite of real food in six weeks.

The therapists came in at the usual time. It was a big job, with all the lines of the machines Nolan was attached to, but they managed to get Nolan to sit at the side of the bed for five minutes. This was another major victory. Later in the afternoon, the nurses put Nolan in the therapy chair for one hour. He sat with his back straight and his legs dropped. As long as he could tolerate sitting in an upright position the nurses encouraged him to do so. Nolan was determined. He wanted out of the hospital and to be back in his home.

Brother John, Brad, Kathy and Brenda visited today. They were thrilled at the progress being made. The Lord showed Himself strong to us. Margie opened up today and shared what she felt early on during Nolan's illness. During her days off she would pray for Nolan's recovery. She would want to call to find out how he was doing. Her professionalism kept her from calling. One day she was driving down the street and an overwhelming feeling came upon her. God was not going to take Nolan home to Him. From that moment forth Margie believed Nolan was going to recover.

Margie shared from her heart, "We have a good nursing team. Everyone has communicated and worked together."

It was another time of the Lord weaving His will into the circumstances, bringing people closer to Him and to each other. I was especially touched by her testimony. It was fresh and straight from the heart. It was that child like faith.

Later that Friday afternoon, Nolan made good to his words – he wanted to go home. In his weakened condition he tried desperately to get out of bed. Tiffany, another day nurse caught him out of the corner of her eye dangling from the side of the bed. He really believed he was able to get up out of bed and walk out of the hospital.

Five nurses emerged at his bedside. They were fearful of any other injury to his body. Nolan had wedged himself between the mattress and the side rail. One of his legs was lying across the top of the rail as if he was just ready to hop out of bed. The five of them moved him back to the center of the bed.

Linda, nose to nose with Nolan, scolded, "You cannot get out of bed. You could hurt yourself and cause possible irreparable damage to your body."

Linda's voice was full of fear. Nolan's eyes were as round and wide as silver dollars. She had made her point.

Nolan was restless that night. When Saturday dawned, Nolan slept all day. He was peaceful. Gnann, our next door neighbor was Nolan's nurse for the day.

I met Tim and Gnann in our neighborhood one day while driving through. Tim was sitting on his front porch passing time. As I noticed him, I also noticed a huge boulder rock sitting in his front yard. We had moved from another state two years previous. A boulder rock was the fashionable item to have in your front yard. I thought for sure these people were "Yankees" just like Nolan and me.

I rolled down the window of the car and called, "I like your rock in your front yard. We had one in our yard in Ohio."

Tim was thrilled and called back, "We have them in our yards where I'm from also. I'm from Michigan and that makes me a "Yankee.""

I laughed, "My husband and I are originally from Iowa, so that makes us "Yankees" too."

We both waved and I went on my way. You never know who you might meet who will become an instrument in your life from the hand of God. Gnann was a regular nurse in the CCU unit. Tim was a per-fusionist at the hospital. Because Gnann was a nurse in CCU and we were their neighbors, Tim stopped in on a regular basis to check on us. It was sweet of them to be so concerned. That was their daily assignment, to do all in their power to save lives. Their concern was only natural and very much a part of what they do.

As I said earlier, the day was peaceful. Dace and Bill, two of the part-time audio crew from the church, stopped in to see Nolan. They prayed for Nolan, visited for awhile with me and then left. In the late afternoon, the food specialists came with a tray of foods to see what textures of foods Nolan could tolerate. It was amazing the care that was taken to bring Nolan back to a normal state of health. All of the staff was hand picked by God. You could see Him in the people that cared for Nolan.

It was Sunday, October 15th. The month was half over. It seemed impossible. The time went fast and yet it did not. Nolan slept well Saturday night. The doctor's orders for the day were no more ativan. Thank you Jesus! Mary, the speech therapist, admin-istered one more swallowing evaluation. Nolan could now eat blended foods.

Jo came today to see her father. Her hectic schedule would only allow her time to come on Sunday afternoon. Jo was a dedicated band student and a dedicated musician. She began her day at 7:00 A.M. When classes were over she went to the band hall, changed her clothes and prepared for band practice. School ended at 2:40 P.M. Band practice began at 3:00 P.M. Her day was over at 5:00 P.M., except for her homework that was reserved for the evening. Jo has been a very busy person for the past two and one half years. This will continue throughout her high school years.

Today would be a day of excitement and relief for her. We had agreed she would come about 2:00 P.M. in the afternoon and relieve me so I could go home to take care of those necessary things that kept piling up. Shortly after I had arrived home the phone rang. It was Jo. She had been talking to her dad. It was the first time they had talked since the morning Nolan went into her room to say "good bye" before he left for surgery.

The Lord always speaks when we are unaware. On August 30th, Nolan went into Jo's room. Nolan shared with Jo how sometimes when surgery is performed the results are not exactly what we expect. He wanted her to know if anything were to happen to him during surgery and he were to go home to be with the Lord that he loved her. This was the careful preparation of her fathers. Jo's earthly father was the vessel and her Heavenly Father had sent the message. This short moment with her father would prove to be a reminder of his love to give her the courage to go forward in the battle.

Jo was relaying her excitement, "Dad and I have been talking!"

I had shared in the previous days when her dad talked, what he had said and how good it was to have him coming back to us. Second-hand information is not the same as the experience firsthand. She had seen and heard for herself. The miracle was unfolding before her eyes. Jo came home from the hospital a different person. She was more herself, joking and laughing at the silliest of situations.

It was Monday, October 16. When I walked into the room, Nolan put out his arms and hugged me. He pulled me to him and kissed me on the lips and cheek. He was more aware and very glad to see me. His nurse said he had been asking for me all morning. During therapy he sat up and balanced himself on the edge of the bed and fed himself ice cream. The nurses stood around his bedside and cheered. Anything and everything Nolan could do was a major step forward. Nolan wanted the Reverend Jody and I to ask Margie for a Pepsi.

He said, "Ask Margie," Margie seemed to have the key to the good stuff.

We asked and Margie came to Nolan's room and asked, "How about a Coke?"

Nolan replied, "Oh yes, I want a Coke."

As Nolan drank his iced Coke, he held Margie's

hand as a gesture of thanks. Earlier in the week the Reverend Jody had brought Nolan an erasable board to write on when it was difficult for us to understand him. He wrote a message to Pastor. Tell Pastor I love him. It was not perfect writing, but the message rang loud and clear. Other than the people visiting each day that he recognized, he remembered Pastor K whom he had not seen since the Sunday before his surgery. People, places and the past was falling into place. Other visitors this day were Rick, Jean, Lisa and Mary and Dean. They all stopped in during their lunch break or after a long hard day at work. They were faithful to the Lord and to us. We were never alone. The Lord saw to it.

As I reflected back to the Friday Nolan was moved to CCU, the thought occurred to me, there was no room for him in SICU, but there was room in CCU. There was no room for Jesus in the inn, but they made room for Him in the stable. All of our lives are precious to God. Where there is no room, He will make room. God's arm is not shortened that it cannot save. What he will do for one he will do for another. Our God is not a respecter of persons. I cannot convey strongly enough that it was not by chance we changed our primary care doctor, we then changed to a different hospital and of course from then on it would be a new staff, a new set of nurses, and a new set of specialists. God's loving hand of care was evident every step of the way regarding Nolan's health care. The timing was

God's. The path was His. And of course the outcome was His divine will.

Nolan was now progressing forward at a strong and steady pace. On Tuesday, October 17, he sat in a regular guest chair for one hour. It took two nurses to get him into the chair and four to put him back in bed. While in bed Nolan would roll and move from side to side. He tried to get out of bed three times. He was determined to gain his strength back. Brad and Pastor Bill visited today during the time Margie was giving Nolan a hair cut. Margie decided Nolan's hair could use some shaping and a good trim. Before her nursing days Margie cut hair for extra food and cash to help support her daughter and herself. She decided she would do this for Nolan. With Brad and Pastor Bill for an audience Nolan began to ham it up. Margie was a talker. While she talked, Nolan would be making faces. Brad and Pastor Bill laughed until tears came to their eyes. Margie's final analysis of the hair trim episode was Nolan having a shampoo, trim and blow dry while eating his snack and entertaining the troops.

The ventilator machine was being used less and less. Nolan had been off the machine today. He sat in the auto flex chair for one and one-half hours. Today he managed to get out of bed and stand up on his own.

Wednesday was much more of the same. He ate a good breakfast. He watched TV while sitting in a chair for two and one-half hours. During therapy he lifted a three-pound bar. It was a good morning. Pastor Gary, a radiologist who happened to be a member at Brownsville, Robin, Katie and Bennie and Hazel visited.

MULTITUDES IN PRAYER – PHASE XI

As of Thursday, October 19, 2000 Nolan had been feeding himself for the previous three days.

He wrote on his erasable board, "Is the pool OK?"

He remembered we have a pool and thought to ask about its condition. Nolan was aware more and more everyday. He wanted me to see if I could get him a new pair of tennis shoes for $9.00. I laughed because he remembered one time when I had found a brand name pair of tennis shoes for $9.00. His mind was becoming clearer and more back into focus on the little things in life.

Dr. C's report for the day was excellent. The perforations in Nolan's intestines would close over time. There was obviously less drainage today then there had been two weeks earlier. Nolan also decided he was going to get better. This was another part of the battle that needed to be overcome. Nolan also had to believe for his recovery.

From 7:45 A.M., Wednesday through today, Nolan had been breathing on his own. During therapy Nolan was standing and taking small steps with the aid of a walker. As he sat he would do leg lifts and arm lifts. The day by day progress was exciting to everyone. The therapists knew Nolan was determined to get better. They allowed Nolan to do what he could, but they would not allow him to overextend himself and create other problems.

We were particularly touched when nurses would take the time to visit on their days off. This was one of those days. Janet, a night nurse was taking a class at the hospital and dropped in to see us. We formed such positive and strong bonds with the nurses. It was difficult later to leave the hospital knowing we might not see them again. They had engraved a place in our hearts that could never be wiped away. Because of the staff's tender, loving care we were forever changed.

Due to Nolan's new found awareness and physical activity, it became necessary once again to call in the over night vigilant troops. Bennie and Hazel and Kathy stayed Wednesday and Thursday nights. I was ever grateful for the constant support and help in our time of need. Nolan now had a trachea mask. Periodically the vent tech would give Nolan a treatment with the trachea mask to loosen up any residue in his lungs.

Brother John, the Reverend Jodi and Jean came to visit in the morning. Nolan had brushed his teeth and had been sitting in the chair for one hour. He wrote on his erasable board, "I want to sit up in bed," and "Jo and Gunter came by." Jo and her friend visited the night before. This was the first time Nolan indicated he remembered from a previous day. Gunter had lost his mother to cancer the year before. He was

exceptionally brave to come with Jo and visit her
Dad. Gunter stood at the end of the bed nearly
motionless. Was this the same man that had just four
months earlier recorded his band? This experience
taught all of us early on that the outcome was strictly
in the Lord's hands. The friends that surrounded Jo
were strong. Gunter was the strongest.

Mary and Pastor Gary visited later in the day.
Mary and I began to share what had happened.
Nolan was asking and with Mary being a nurse, there
was no better time to tell the story.

Mary began, "Do you remember you came into
the hospital for a hiatal hernia surgery?"

Nolan was not certain he remembered the hernia
surgery.

Mary continued, "You developed sepsis and had a
fever of 108 degrees for several hours. Pancreatitis
set in and an abscess had formed beginning at the
pancreas. It grew behind the stomach and continued
to the front of the stomach. The abscess was surgi-
cally removed."

A look of disbelief and shock came over Nolan.
He wanted to hear it again. Mary carefully chose her
words and repeated what had happened. That was
enough for now, in fact it was more than enough for
Nolan to begin to comprehend. I was especially
grateful to have Mary there when Nolan began asking about his condition. God met this need in such a
reassuring manner. I could tell Nolan was comforted
in knowing Mary was there for us. It was important

to God to have the appropriate people in place at the right time. Jesus sits at the right hand of the Father ever interceding for us.

From October 21st to October 31st there was much of the same progress. Margie also went over what had happened. It was beginning to sink in. With the second surgery the incision was left open. Nolan's body was extended to the point that the incision could not be closed. A plastic wrap was placed over the open area. Dr. C waited until Nolan's swollen condition began to subside.

Nolan asked, "Which doctor will be releasing me?"

Margie responded with reassuring words, "Dr. C will release you. He's gone for a few days. He will see you just as soon as he returns."

At this point Nolan's voice could be heard more consistently even though the trachea was still in place. Dr. W would order the trachea to be plugged on Monday.

On Sunday October 22nd, Nolan was moved from CCU to PCU. Dr. R, Dr. C's associate, wrote the orders for Nolan to be moved because of his insistence. Nolan wanted to go home. As the light in the tunnel became brighter for Nolan the doctors' personalities blossomed.

Nolan insisted, "When can I go home?"

Dr. R with a teasing sincerity, "You can go home today!"

With a wide grin he quickly added, "Just kidding!"

I laughed until tears came to my eyes. Those moments brought such comic relief. Every time I think of that moment I laugh. This particular group of doctors was especially light hearted. It appeared they understood that laughter was good medicine for the soul. Nolan's recovery was a major victory for them. In the beginning they also knew Nolan's recovery was in God's hands.

It was difficult for the CCU staff to let Nolan go. They had become fond of us and of the many friends that visited. In the darkest moments, we were the easiest people to deal with. We were not a burden to them, but a joy. We encouraged the staff whenever the opportunity arose. Throughout the days and weeks, we became their strength and they were God's manifestation of strength to us.

When Dr. C returned and entered Nolan's new room he beamed with excitement.

As Dr. C reached forward to shake Nolan's hand he said, "Hey man, I heard you got moved!"

Nolan responded with the only thought on his mind, "Can I go home?"

Dr. C grinning from ear to ear, "I'm just so glad you are alive!"

As Dr. C reassured Nolan he would be going home soon he asked, "Oh by the way, how is the reflux?"

Nolan asked, "What is that?"

Dr. C looked at me with a big smile, "Well, that is

working!"

Nolan spent Monday opening mail he had received while in the hospital and reading audio magazines to catch up on the latest news. He called five times from the hospital between 6:30 A.M. through 7:40 A.M. when I left to go to the hospital. He stood up on his own and held on to the table. During therapy he walked two doors down the hall and back. He was particularly hungry and ate a full breakfast and lunch. Later that day, Jo and I planned a surprise dinner party for the Reverend Jodi. Mr. John grilled chicken in the way only Mr. John can grill. Jo bought balloons and a card that reflected our gratitude for the time Ms. Jodi spent with us. At the age of twenty-six the Reverend was strong in the Lord. During Nolan's stay in the hospital she proved herself faithful. She belongs completely to Jesus.

October 24, 2000 was the anniversary of our eighteenth-year of marriage. I arrived at the hospital to find six beautiful roses with a card and candy. The roses were a burnt peach color, the color of my bride maids' dresses. The card was the kind of card that only Nolan could pick out and the candy was my favorite. How could this be? I had to catch my breath before I could thank Nolan. The Reverend Jodi had been at the hospital early that morning. She was busy helping Nolan prepare this surprise for our anniversary. These little details truly reflect the heart of God. His hand was in it, because He wanted this to be a special time for me.

Nolan's trachea was capped at 8:40 A.M. I had called my mother before I left the house that morning, but her line was busy. By the time I reached the hospital, she had called thinking I would be there. Much to her surprise Nolan answered the phone. My mother was shocked and excited to hear his voice. The last time she had seen Nolan he was unresponsive. Later I learned she had immediately called every family member to tell them the good news. The response was one of two, either there was extreme awe or disbelief. Through her tears and sobs, my mother told each family member of her conversation with Nolan. A feeling of relief overwhelmed her. She was seeing specific answers to prayer.

Later that day, a crowd of co-workers from Brownsville came to visit. As soon as Nolan's trachea had been capped he called Brenda's office and left a message on her answering machine. With tears in their eyes, Pastor Gary, Brad, Brenda, Sandy and Bill H. stood at the end of Nolan's bed in awe of God. They laughed, they cried and they just stood there looking at Nolan and the wonderful miracle God had wrought.

Two days later, Dr. W removed the trachea plug with a promise the trachea incision would close within two to three days. The fistula drain and catheter to Nolan's bladder were removed. Test results were coming back quickly and with positive results. Nolan was now going twice a day to the therapy gym with Christy and James.

On October 29th, Nolan was finally able to take a shower. It was a simple pleasure of life. He was transferred to the fourth floor of the hospital. The doctors were getting ready to release him. During these last three days nurses and staff members came to say "good-bye" to Nolan.

With wide teary eyes Dawn, Sophia and Margie would come and say, "You look so good and you are doing so well."

They would laugh for joy, stand motionless with the awe of the miracle God had performed and weep with an overwhelming sense of accomplishment. They had done their part and God had revealed Himself to them.

Dr. C saw Mary earlier in the day and she told him, "Nolan looks good!"

The expression on Dr. C's face and the tone of his voice indicated to me that he valued Mary's opinion as a nurse. They had become veterans in this medical war.

Dr. C made his final pronouncement over Nolan, "Nothing was going to happen, Nolan can go home."

As Dale and I gathered Nolan's belongings others stopped in to say their "good-byes." Dr. W was just glad Nolan was going home. Janet stopped in and shared a few funny stories of Nolan's stay in CCU. We called Dr. C's nurse, Ginny, to schedule an appointment in Dr. C's office.

As Ginny listened to Nolan's voice on the phone she responded, "This is the best phone call I have ever received!"

Nolan was discharged on Wednesday, October 31, 2000 at 1:00 P.M.

Epilogue

࿓

One day in mid-October, with my mind reflecting on the previous weeks, I thought to myself, "How did we believe?"

God showed me in the spirit just how He ordered the circumstances. There was the Father, the Son and The Holy Spirit present at all times. The multitudes covered us in prayer. A wall of fire surrounded us as promised in Zechariah 2:5 – "For I," saith the Lord, will be unto her a wall of fire round about and will be the glory in the midst of her." Brother John led the way, while Pastor Gary confessed that Nolan would take up his bed and walk and Mary walked by my side all the way. Jo and I were sheltered in the midst of the three. The Glory of God was in the midst of us. There was a thread of joy and peace brought by the presence of the Holy Spirit.

I believed because God would not allow me to think anything other than everything was going to be alright. The very fact that God was present from start to finish indicated to me that everything was going to turn out for the good of all.

Our trial impacted many lives. Those who prayed became better prayers. Those who believed gained more faith. Those who trusted God for the outcome gained more trust in Him. God's purpose and plans always have a ripple effect. When His plans are in motion it is like a set of dominos. The first domino falls and then the next domino, until all have fallen. The last fallen domino indicates His plans are complete. During the process, lives have been forever changed and His perfect will has been established.

The following weeks and months were times of continued healing. There were follow up visits to Dr. C. He was always glad to see Nolan, marveling at God's hand of grace upon him. When Dr. C released Nolan from the hospital there were no prescriptions for medications Nolan had been taking. There was nothing prescribed for high blood pressure, reflux or ulcers and no cholesterol medicine. He was free. For the first time, free from pain because of ulcers, discomfort from acid build up in his stomach and free from pain in his chest.

Everywhere we would go people would marvel at what God had done for Nolan. With their eyes wide and standing speechless, many would stare at Nolan in awe. Everyone knew the odds were against him to survive, but everyone also knew God had turned the circumstances around. Glory to God, He has shown

Himself strong. Now, it would be up to those who did not have a personal relationship with the Lord and those who were "kind of/sort of" walking with Him, to choose whom they would serve.

As for Nolan, Jo and me – Acts 20:24 – as the Apostle Paul so eloquently stated,

"But none of these things move me, neither count I my life dear unto myself, so that I might finish my course with joy, and the ministry which I have received of the Lord Jesus, to testify the gospel of the grace of God."

BLESSINGS TO YOU!

Nolan, Jan and Jo Pauley

ST. JOHN'S LUTHERAN CHURCH
5802 Franconia Road
Alexandria, Virginia 22310

RETURN REQUESTED